Jewi.

Illustrated by Brenda Rae Eno

Chronicle Books ♦ San Francisco

Printed in Hong Kong

ISBN: 0-87701-667-4

Distributed in Canada by
Raincoast Books, 112 East 3rd Ave.,
Vancouver, B.C. V5T 1 CB

10 9 8 7 6 5 4 3 2 1

Chronicle Books
275 Fifth Street
San Francisco, California 94103

Better an ounce of luck
than a pound of gold.

If you want to be a barber,
practice on someone else's beard.

Uphill we always climb with
caution, downhill we dash, carefree.

It is better to suffer in Hell
with a wise man than frolic
in Paradise with a fool.

Too much good food is worse
than too little bad food.

If my grandmother had wheels
she'd be a bus.

I felt sorry I had no shoes until
I saw the man who had no feet.

One drop of love can
create a sea of tears.

Speech is silver, silence is golden.

If you lie with dogs
you get up with fleas.

If you quarrel with the rabbi,
make peace with the bartender.

When schnapps goes in,
judgment goes out.

With money in your pocket,
you are wise and you are handsome
and you sing well too.

A glutton for cake
often loses the bread.

The apple doesn't fall
far from the tree.

Old friends, like old wines,
don't lose their flavor.

A word that is aptly spoken
is like an apple of gold
in a setting of carved silver.

So many hymns—
and so few noodles.

If velvet and silk hang in your closet,
you can step out in rags.

A whole fool is half a prophet.

One is a lie, two are lies,
but three is politics.

From your lips to God's ear.

Better the bite of a friend
than the kiss of an enemy.

Cheap borsht is a blessing
to the toothless.

Hurry and eat, hurry and drink,
for this world is like a wedding feast
from which we must soon depart.

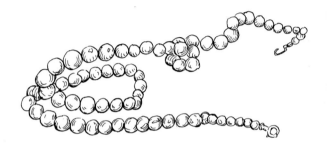

Wisdom is more precious than pearls.

Guests, like fish, begin to
smell on the third day.

The man who is destined to drown
will drown in a glass of water.

Those who live near a waterfall
do not hear its roar.

When the sin is sweet,
repentance is not so bitter.

It is best not to live in a city
run by scholars.

My pen is my harp and my lyre;
my library is my garden
and my orchard.

You can't swap jokes
with the Angel of Death.

We are too soon old
and too late wise.

The egg of today is better
than the hen of tomorrow.

In time, even a bear
can learn to dance.

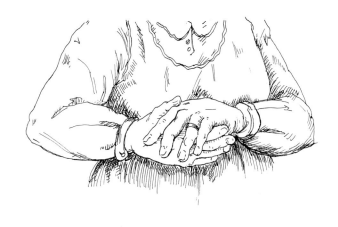

Never waste good agony.

As you are at seven,
so you are at seventy.

Fortune is a wheel that
turns with great speed.

A worm in a jar of horseradish
thinks he is in Paradise.

God loves the poor and helps the rich.

Any man surrounded by dwarfs
looks like a giant.

Even an angel cannot do
two things at the same time.

Be not in a hurry, like the almond,
first to bloom and last to ripen;
be rather like the mulberry,
last to blossom and first to ripen.

44

If not for the light,
there would be no shadow.

Peace is to man
what yeast is to dough.

Don't enter the forest
if you fear leaves.

There are three things you cannot
hide: coughing, poverty, and love.

Gossip is silenced with gold.

It is better to eat vegetables and
fear no creditors than to eat duck
and hide from them.

Some prefer vinegar
and some prefer wine.

Gray hair is a glorious crown
won by a righteous life.

You can't chew with
someone else's teeth.

If the heart is bitter,
sugar in the mouth won't help.

Always marry for love—but
it's as easy to fall in love with
a rich person as a poor one.

All the world is on
the tip of the tongue.

Those who can't dance say
the musicians can't keep time.

Bright eyes gladden the heart;
good news fattens the bones.